TYPES OF BEETLES

Weevil

Ground Beetle

Tiger Beetle

Stag Beetle

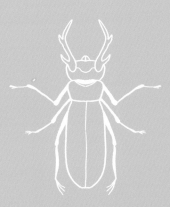

Scarab Beetle

Skin Beetle

Ladybug

Jewel Beetle

Rhinoceros Beetle

A Young Naturalist

Born in 1809, Charles Darwin grew up loving nature and was obsessed with collecting plants. He found school very boring and spent his free time collecting beetles and learning the art of taxidermy.

Charles made friends with a botany professor at Cambridge named John Stevens Henslow. In 1831, John helped Charles get a job as a naturalist to survey South America.

The Famous Journey

Charles set sail on the *HMS Beagle* and ended up traveling all over the world to study flora and fauna. The epic journey took five whole years! He encountered all kinds of amazing animals, plants, and fossils, which led him to make many incredible discoveries.

He wrote a lot of papers and books over the course of his trip and for years afterwards about his theories on natural selection, adaptation, and, most famously—evolution.

Father of Evolution

Charles passed away at the age of 73, surrounded by his beloved wife and children. He was celebrated as the first person to make incredible breakthroughs in evolutionary science and to convince the world that it was possible that humans evolved from apes!

Charles Darwin is known as the first person to discover evolution, but what about the lesser known SECOND person, the one who helped to prove that those theories were true?

This book is dedicated to my cool friends: Dana, Sarah, and Louise.

It's not dedicated to my stinky cat, Gordon, who peed on my first draft.

This Book Belongs To

_____

Published by Yeehoo Press
6540 Lusk Blvd, Ste C152, San Diego, CA 92121
www.yeehoopress.com

Edited by Jiahui Zhu
Designed by Si Ye
Original concept by Zhiqiao Wang
Supervised by Luyang Xue
Library of Congress Control Number: 2022931496
ISBN: 978-1-953458-38-4
Printed in China First Edition
1 2 3 4 5 6 7 8 9 10

THE SECOND IN THE WORLD

to Discover Evolution: *Alfred Russel Wallace*

By Farren Phillips

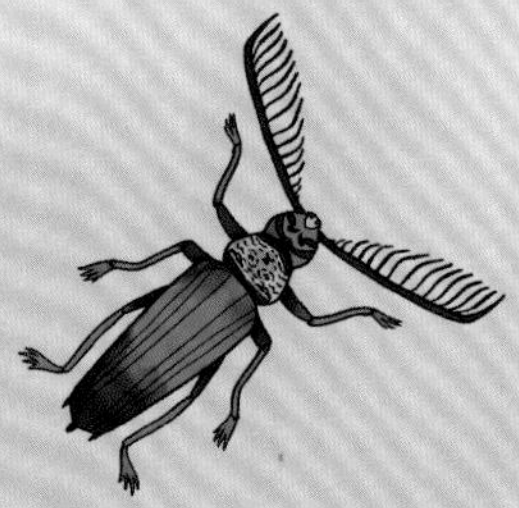

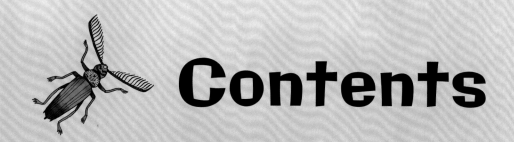

Contents

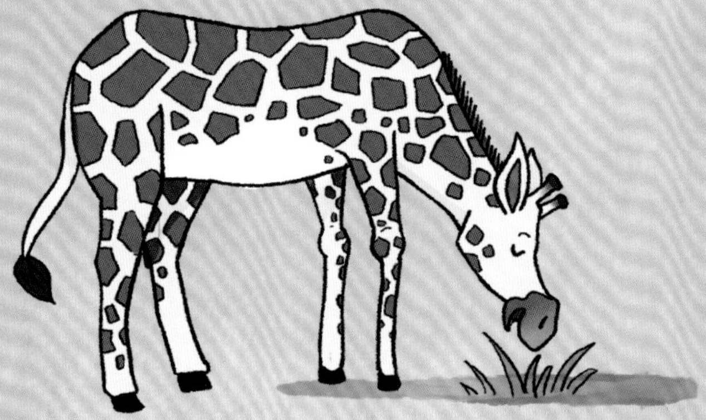

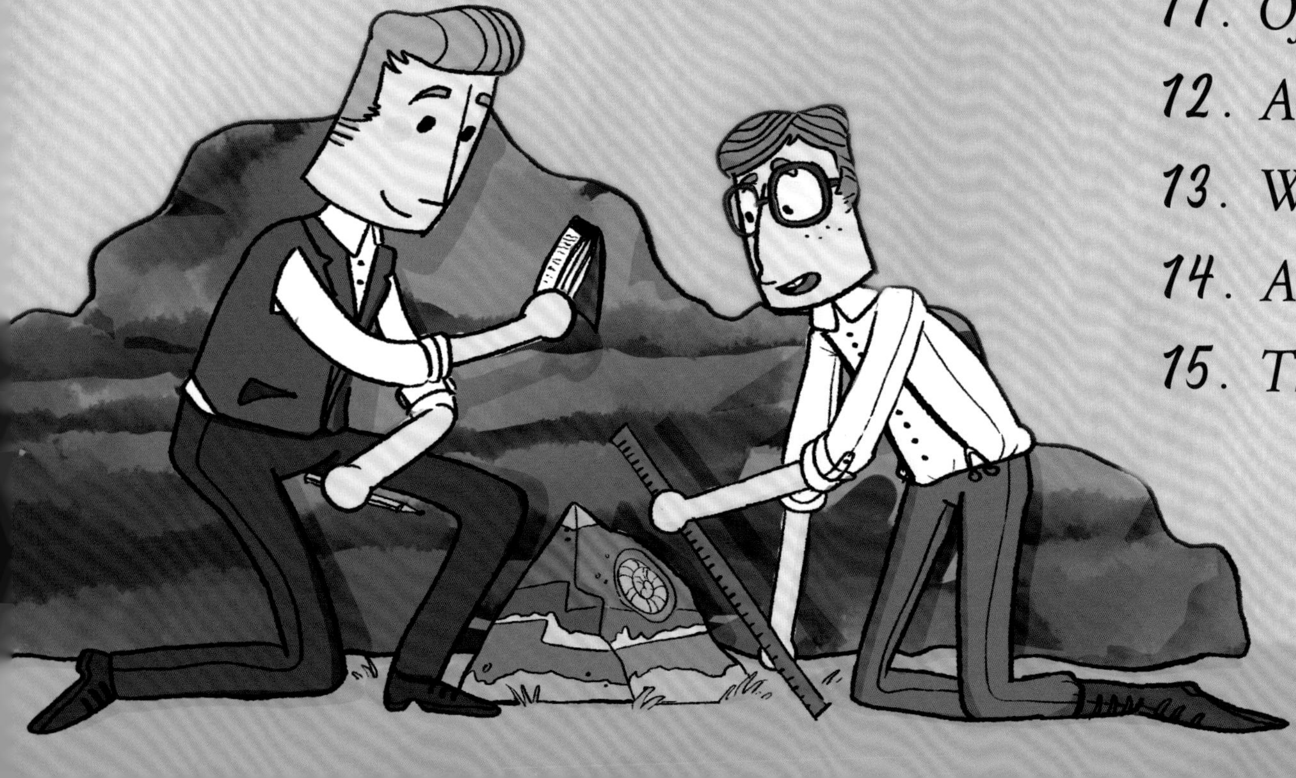

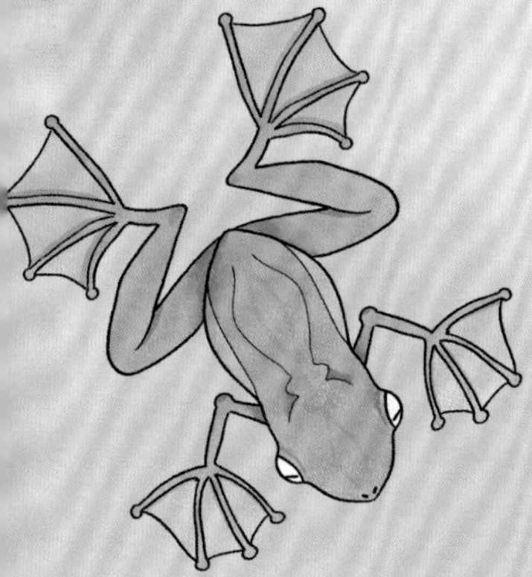

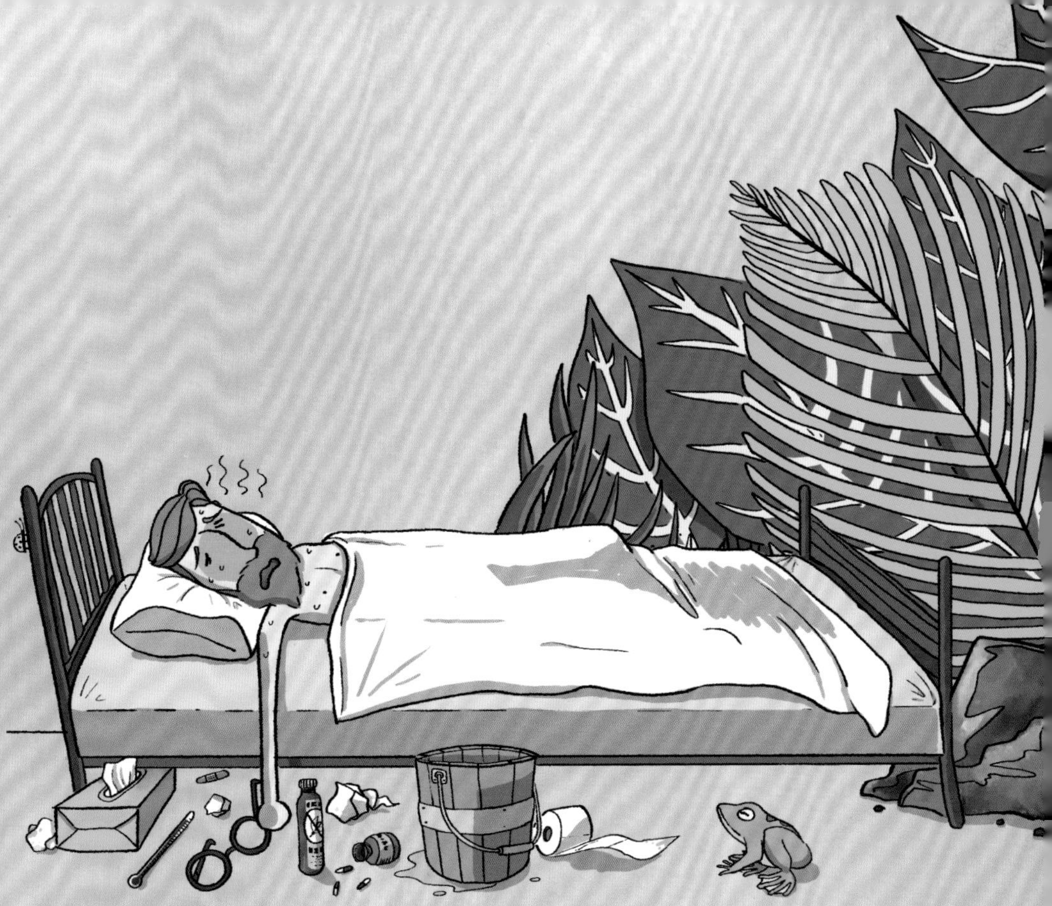

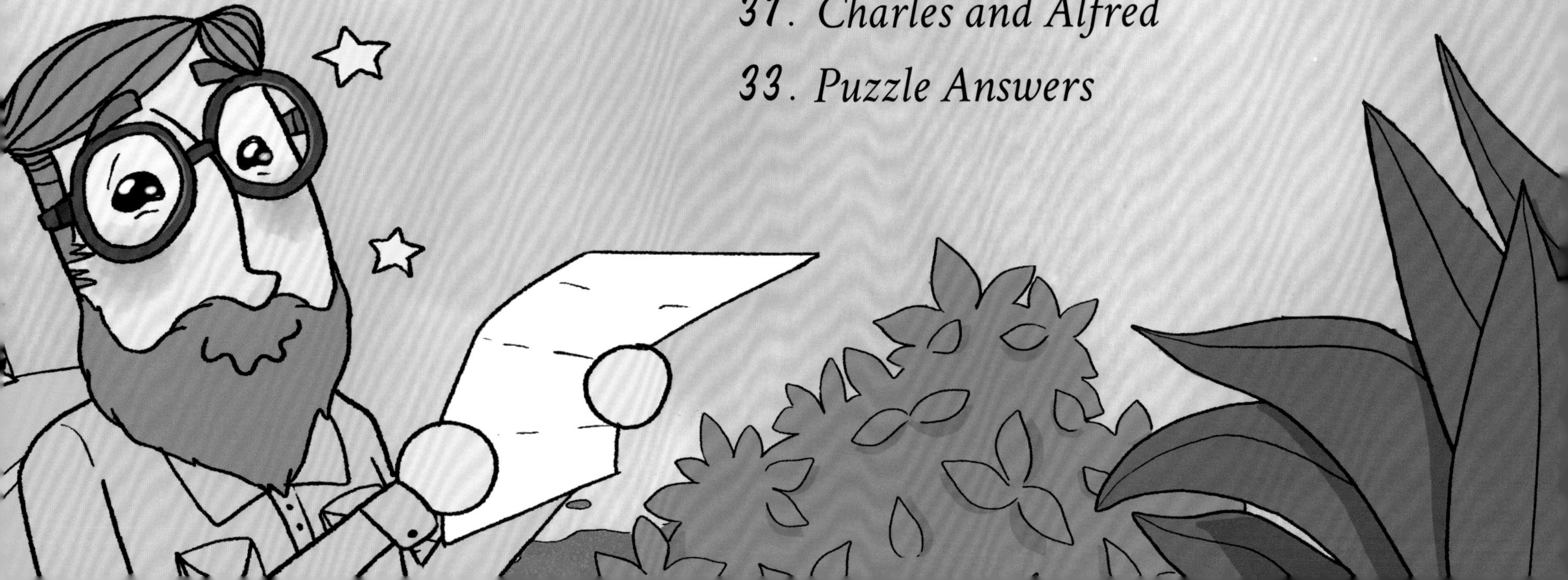

EARLY DAYS OF ALFRED

Born in 1823 in a small town in Wales called Usk, Alfred had eight siblings, and they lived a modest life without very much money. When Alfred was five, his family moved to Hertford in England. He went to school until he was 14, then got his first job to help his family with money.

14 might sound young, but many people left school young in the 19th century, or didn't go to school at all! In fact, the term "teenager" wasn't first used until 100 years later in the 1920s. Before that, you were seen as a child until you were mature enough to work, and then you were an adult! No in-between. Children could start working as young as five years old.

ALFRED'S FIRST JOB

Alfred left school to start surveying for his older brother. He learned many skills such as measuring land and hills and distinguishing types of rocks and fossils. He found that he really loved working outdoors and became very enthusiastic about nature.

He then went on to use his skills to teach drawing, mapmaking, and surveying at the Collegiate School in Leicester, where he spent his free time studying in the library and attending lectures. Alfred read huge amounts about natural history, history, political economy, and the works of Charles Darwin.

Alfred loved to learn new things, especially about science, and always had his nose in a book. He became very interested in the theory of transmutation.

TRANSMU-WHAT?!

Transmutation was the scientific theory tha animals could change their features over time. But why? Well that's what no one was sure of. A scientist named Jean-Baptiste Pierre Antoine de Monet, chevalier de Lamarck dedicated his life to trying to answer this question, but he never really nailed the answer. Jean-Baptiste thought that all forms of life were created by "spontaneous generation," which means he believed that living things could pop up anywhere, even when there had been no life before. He theorized that sometimes these new animals would come with important changes that helped them be healthier and happier where they lived.

One of the most classic examples of Jean-Baptiste's takes on things is how he thought giraffes got their long necks. Fossils show that giraffes, once upon a time, had shorter necks, a bit like horses. Jean-Baptiste theorized that, because giraffes needed to eat food located high up, they began to stretch their necks. As they continued to reach for lush greenery, they stretched and stretched until they became the long-necked beasts we know today.

We know now that Jean-Baptiste was on the right track ... but his theory was a little off the mark. What really happened was that some giraffes had slightly longer necks than others, and those giraffes had a natural advantage and went on to produce more offspring. Over generations, those long-necked genes adapted and were passed on because the longer the giraffe's neck, the more food they could get and the more likely they were to mate.

CRAZY COLLECTORS

When Alfred was 21 years old, he made a new friend at the library named Henry Walter Bates. Henry had an incredible collection of insects, and it inspired Alfred to start his own. The two of them would spend hours hunting the tiny critters together.

Can you find all 14 creepy crawlies hiding on this page?

Journey to Brazil

Alfred desperately wanted to visit foreign lands to search for undiscovered species of insects, so in 1848, he and Henry organized a trip to Brazil. Their plan was to collect specimens of insects and sell the duplicates to museums back in England to pay for their trip. But he also hoped to find evidence of transmutation there.

Museums like to have expansive collections of preserved plants, animals, and insect bodies to study and exhibit. Back in those days, they would pay naturalists to bring them these specimens.

Warning Coloration

They noticed that there were many insects like caterpillars and beetles with bright colors and patterns on their bodies. This was strange because surely that would make them easier targets for predators. Years later, Alfred realized that the bright colors on these insects were to warn predators that they were poisonous and bad tasting.

Henry made a huge discovery around warning coloration too—he realized that sometimes harmless insects mimicked the colors and patterns of noxious insects to pretend to be poisonous and avoid predators. This is known as Batesian mimicry, which was named after him.

This is a monarch butterfly. See how its bright orange and black wings make it stick out against its green environment? Predators are able to see it easily, but the bright colors tell them that it's poisonous and bitter to eat, so they leave it alone. No one wants a mouthful of something yucky!

6

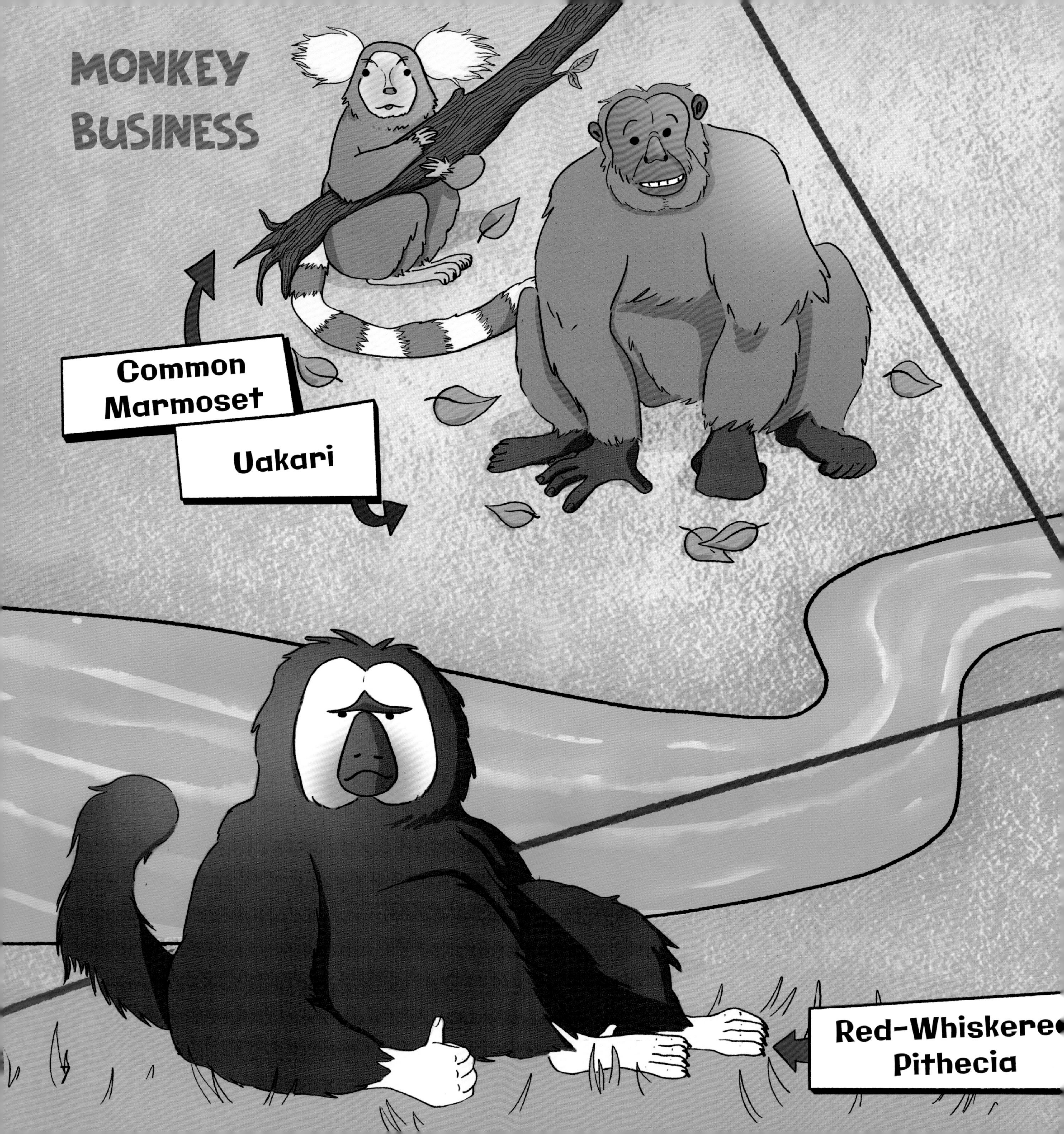
MONKEY BUSINESS
Common Marmoset
Uakari
Red-Whiskered Pithecia

Alfred noticed that different species of monkeys lived on opposite sides of a large river, the Rio Negro. At the lower end of the riverbank, on the north side, he found common marmosets and uakaris, and on the south side he found red-whiskered pithecia. Higher up the river on the banks of the north side, he found red-faced spider monkeys, and on the south side, brown woolly monkeys. The different monkeys stayed only within their zones, as if separated by an invisible line.

Red-Faced Spider Monkey

Brown Woolly Monkey

Alfred theorized that the monkeys had all started as the same species but then changed over multiple generations, and somehow, the changes all made them better able to survive their different local environments.

8

GOING IT ALONE

Eventually, Henry and Alfred decided to continue their adventures separately. Alfred spent three years exploring the Amazon rainforest, collecting thousands of specimens, and mapping parts of the Amazon River.

DISASTER STRIKES!

A nightmare happened! In 1852, Alfred decided to bring his findings home to the UK. The ship he was traveling on, the *Helen*, caught fire and sank. Alfred had to watch his precious specimens and years of notes sink to the bottom of the ocean. Alfred and the crew were stranded on a lifeboat for 10 days before they were rescued.

Imagine being a scuba diver and one day coming across jars of insects and birds at the bottom of the sea. Wouldn't that be a confusing discovery?

PICKING UP THE PIECES

Alfred wasn't so easily defeated, though. He made it home safely and picked himself back up, writing many books and articles about everything he learned in the Amazon. He established himself as a naturalist in England and started to plan his next adventure.

OFF TO ASIA

In 1854, having planned an even more adventurous trip than the last, Alfred decided to set out across the sea to travel all over Asia in search of new specimens and discoveries. Indonesia and Malaysia were known for their huge jungles full of exotic birds and insects, and Alfred just had to see it for himself.

ALI WALLACE

As he explored the jungles of the Malay Archipelago, Alfred had a team of helpers: guides who knew the land, cooks, sailors, porters, and hunters to kill and skin specimens. One of Alfred's most trusted helpers was a teenage boy named Ali from Sarawak Borneo (which we now know as Malaysia!).

Despite being only 15, Ali was extremely intelligent and hard working. It's thought that he may have even collected or helped collect the majority of the bird specimens that Alfred brought back to the UK. Not much was written about Ali and he never got the recognition he deserved, but we know that Alfred could never have made the discoveries he did without the assistance of his most faithful companion. Ali enjoyed working with Alfred so much that he later gave himself the surname of Wallace in Alfred's honor.

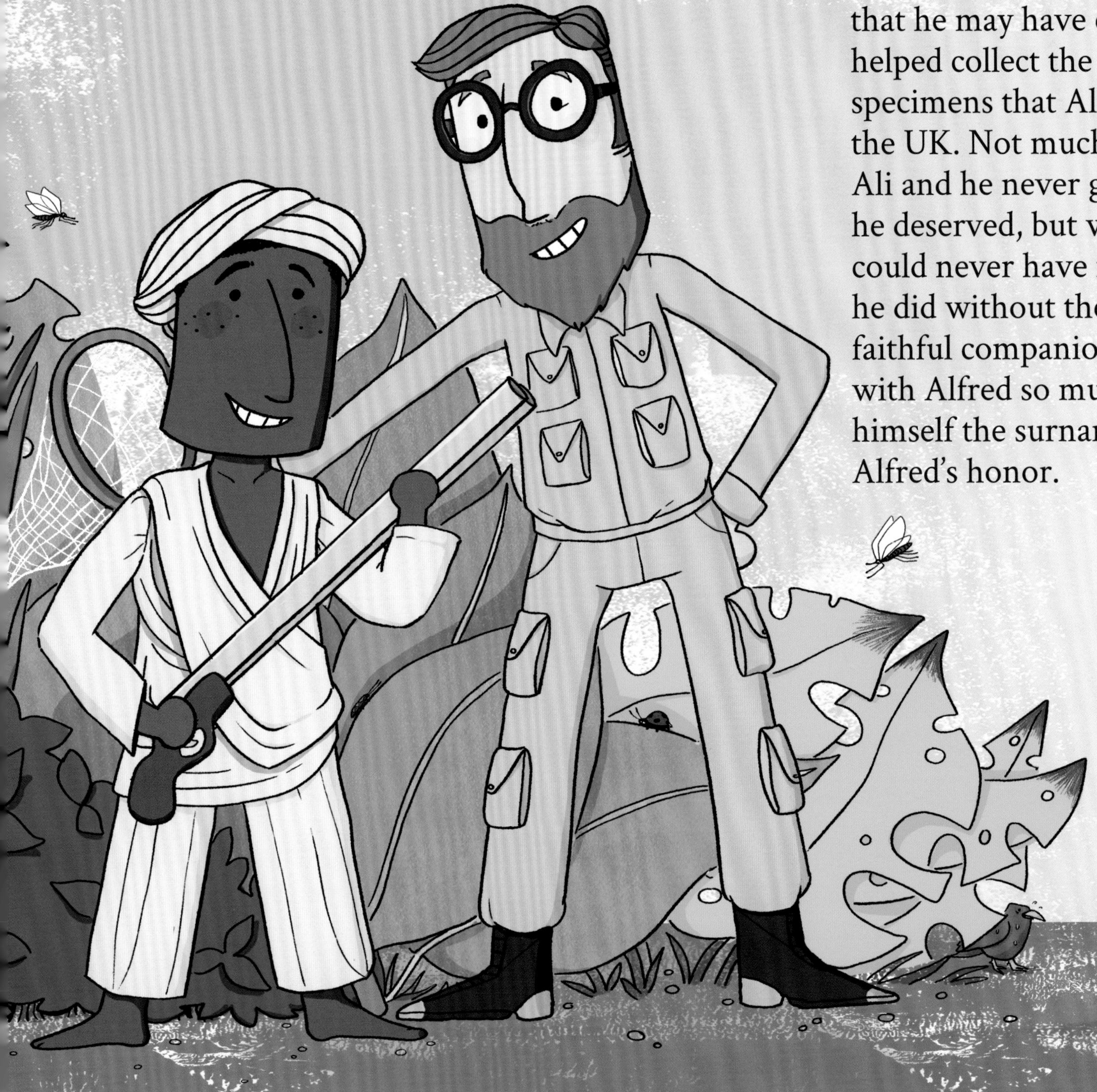

WHAT A COLLECTION!

Alfred's journey lasted eight years and he traveled more than 10,000 miles. Over that time, he collected almost 110,000 insects, 7,500 shells, 8,050 bird skins, and 410 mammals. There are nearly 10,000 different species of birds in the world, and Alfred discovered just over 2% of them. That's 246 types of birds that no one had ever documented before!

Some of Alfred's collections have escaped! Can you help by finding them out?

ALFRED AND DARWIN

Alfred was becoming more established in the science world through his research and started to converse with Charles Darwin via letters. Alfred and Charles had similar ideas and theories regarding natural selection, and they were both passionately working towards proving the theory of transmutation. The main difference between them was that Charles was a few years older and far more established in the scientific community. Plus, they didn't agree on everything. Charles theorized that successful mating in animals was not just limited to the best survival assets, but also more attractive features in the animals too, like how peacocks may choose their partner based on their impressive tail display. Alfred had doubts about this—he felt that survival was the more important feature and that physical attraction was only a human thing.

THE WALLACE LINE

One of the huge discoveries Alfred made was the Wallace Line, an invisible line across the Malay Archipelago separating Asia and Australia. Millions of years ago, these continents were joined together as one huge continent. Back then, animals could move about this big landmass easily and plants could grow all over. When Asia and Australia became separated by an ocean, the animals left on each continent were now stuck, and over thousands of years they adapted and evolved to fit their specific location.

For example, in Southeast Asia you might find elephants, but you'll never find them in Australia. In Australia, you might find echidnas, but you'll never find them in Asia.

Ancestors of elephants thrived in the cool jungles of Asia, full of greenery to eat, but they became extinct in the desert lands of Australia. Ancestors of echidnas coped well with the surroundings of Australia, but couldn't compete with the predators in the jungles of Asia. Some other examples are tigers and rhinos in Asia and kangaroos and platypuses in Australia.

SICKNESS AND SOLUTIONS

In 1855, in a paper called, "On the Law Which Has Regulated the Introduction of New Species," Alfred raised a question: Why do some things die and other things live? Over the next few years, he began eagerly seeking the answer.

In 1858, he caught jungle fever on his travels (which today we call malaria, a serious disease spread by mosquito bites). He was very ill and bedridden for weeks, and he spent that time deep in thought about his research while his body raged with fever.

He'd heard of an economist named Thomas Robert Malthus, who most famously theorized that the human population would often grow faster than the food supply, and so to have the most efficient population, there needed to be limits on reproduction. This idea got Alfred thinking that maybe the theory applied to animals and plants too.

While stuck in bed, he was thinking about the animal kingdom and the effects of disease, famine, and predators.

It suddenly dawned on him that in the struggle for survival, the healthiest, strongest, and swiftest animals were always going to be the ones who survived the longest . . . and thus go on to breed and spread their genes further.

Over generations, whole species would change depending on the features that helped them survive the best in their surroundings.

DARWIN GETS THE MESSAGE

Alfred excitedly wrote down all his thoughts and sent a letter to Charles Darwin to read and to send onto Sir Charles Lyell, a renowned geologist. Darwin was shocked and a little horrified because Alfred had figured out almost the exact same thing as he had written 14 years ago but not yet published.

Darwin hadn't published his paper on natural selection because he was worried the scientific community wouldn't take the ideas very well. It's likely that Alfred was nervous about this too, and that's why he sent his paper to Darwin rather than sending it off to be published.

In 1857, Darwin was writing to an American botanist named Asa Gray and when he mentioned his research and beliefs, the ideas weren't met very well. The bad response left Darwin feeling very discouraged, so he begged the fellow scientist not to tell anyone about his ideas out of fear, worried that if word got around that he was a believer in such controversial topics, the scientific community would dismiss him before he could provide solid evidence for the concept of evolution.

Darwin, Lyell, and a botanist named Joseph Hooker got together and concocted a plan to announce Darwin's theory of evolution to the Linnean Society, using Alfred's paper as supportive evidence. Unfortunately, the chairman of the society didn't agree with their ideas at all and didn't want to hear a word of it.

Darwin was motivated by Alfred's ideas, and even though he was turned down at first, he finally took a brave step and went on to publish *The Origin of Species* in 1859. It took many years of controversy in the scientific community for the idea of evolution to become widely accepted, but this was the first huge step.

Alfred, while all this was happening, was still out in the Malay Archipelago continuing his research. He didn't even know that the Linnean Society had seen his work! When Darwin wrote back to tell him, he was thrilled, even though the meeting hadn't gone well. Alfred was just excited to share his findings on evolution.

EVOLUTION

Many animals we know and love today shared common ancestors with other very different creatures. For example, your pet dog shares the same ancestral lineage as vicious gray wolves! A long time ago, the world had many kinds of wolves such as dire wolves, megafaunal wolves, and cave wolves.

Over time, groups of wolves adapted to their surroundings and changed over generations. Today, there are more than 30 subspecies of gray wolves alone. The dogs we share our homes with originated from isolated gene pools of early wolf cubs that were domesticated by humans.

Hi, Great-Uncle Steve!

ROAR

As another funny example of unlikely animal relations, it's believed that chickens shared ancestors with the tyrannosaurus rex.

Can you match up which animals on the right you think shared ancestors with the animals on the left?

Elephant

Horse

Dolphin

Pig

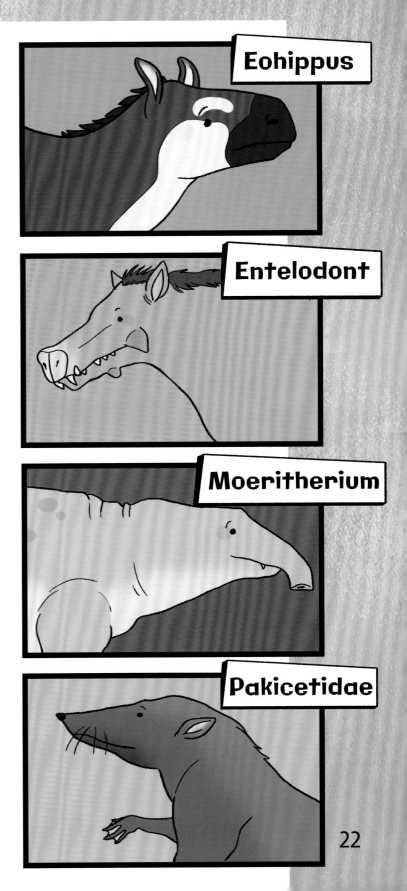

Eohippus

Entelodont

Moeritherium

Pakicetidae

HOW IT WORKS

Let's look at foxes as an example. Foxes live all over the place, from the Arctic to the desert. Once, a long time ago, they all looked fairly similar.

In the Arctic, they hunted in the snow for lemmings, and in the desert, they hunted in the sand for lizards.

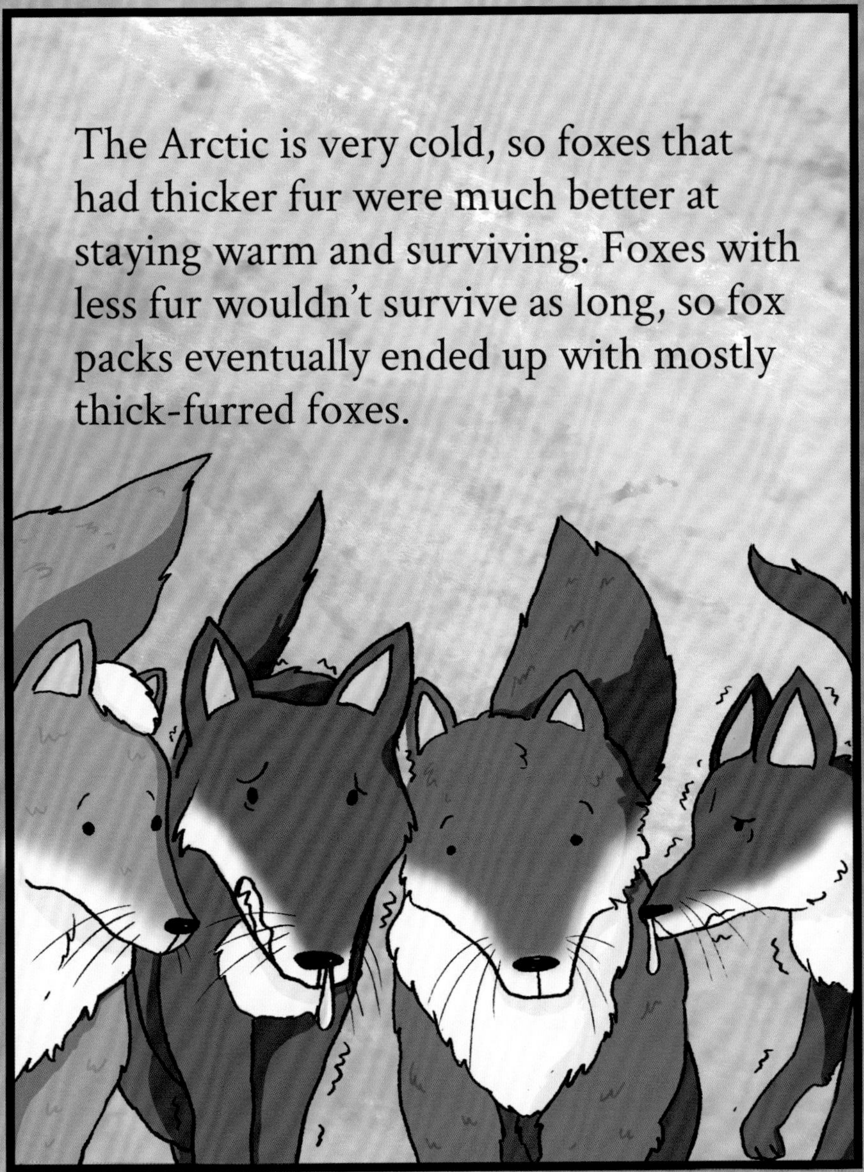
The Arctic is very cold, so foxes that had thicker fur were much better at staying warm and surviving. Foxes with less fur wouldn't survive as long, so fox packs eventually ended up with mostly thick-furred foxes.

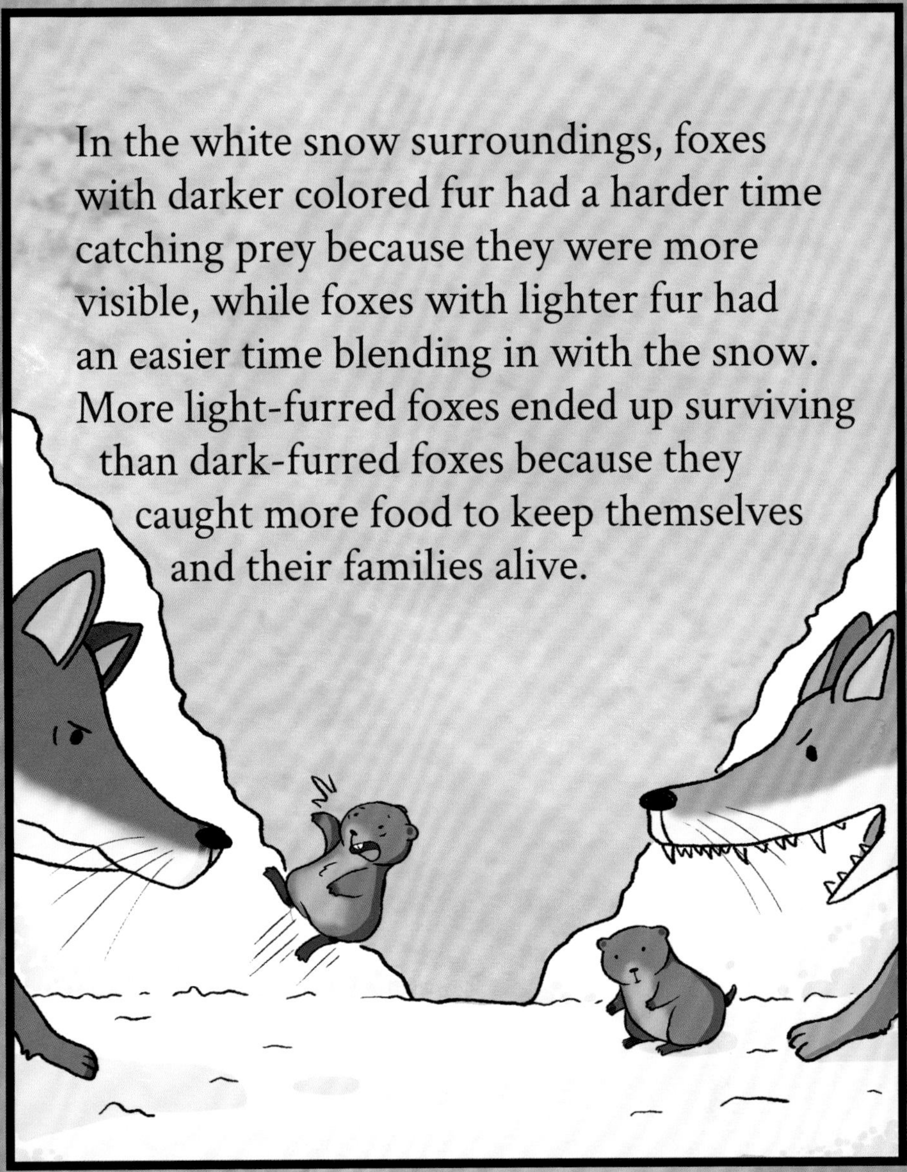
In the white snow surroundings, foxes with darker colored fur had a harder time catching prey because they were more visible, while foxes with lighter fur had an easier time blending in with the snow. More light-furred foxes ended up surviving than dark-furred foxes because they caught more food to keep themselves and their families alive.

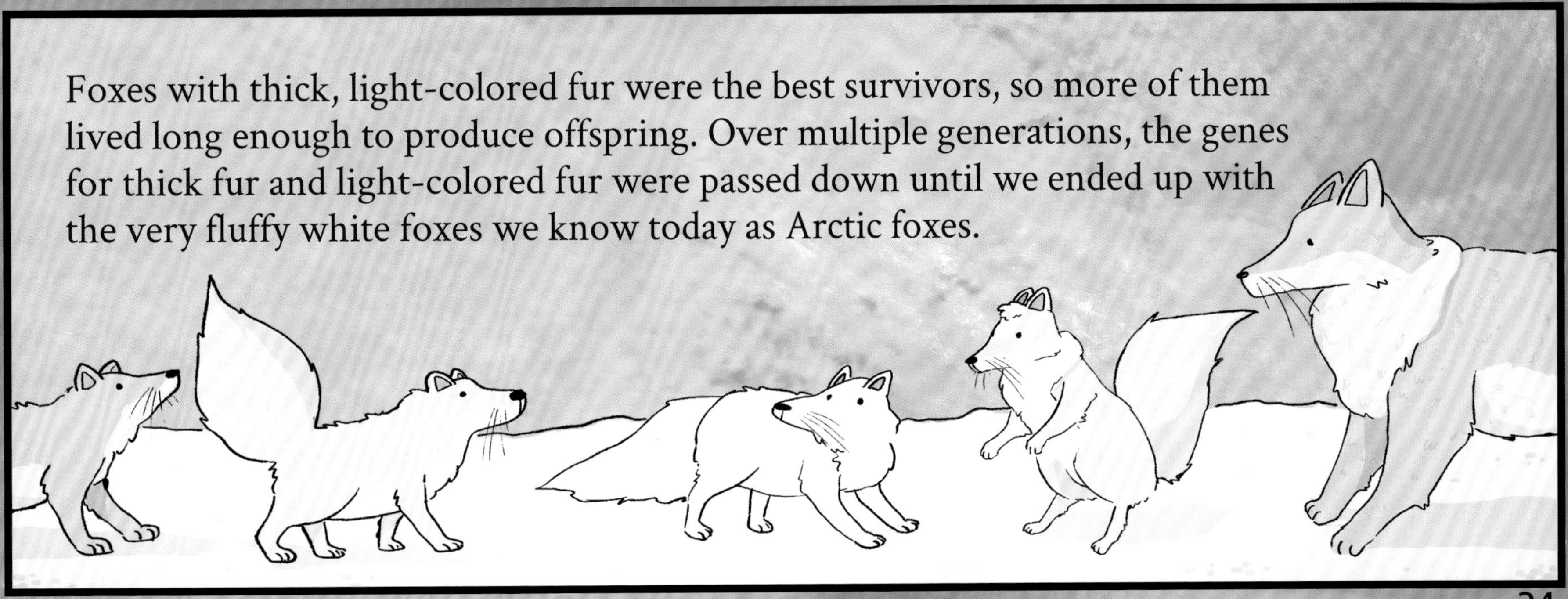
Foxes with thick, light-colored fur were the best survivors, so more of them lived long enough to produce offspring. Over multiple generations, the genes for thick fur and light-colored fur were passed down until we ended up with the very fluffy white foxes we know today as Arctic foxes.

The desert, on the other hand, is very hot. Foxes with thicker fur had a much harder time controlling their body heat in the sweltering sun and were far more prone to overheating than foxes with shorter fur. So these fox packs eventually ended up with lots of short-furred foxes.

Dark coats weren't such a problem for the desert foxes blending in with sand and dirt, but their prey, lizards, were very good at staying hidden under the sand. Desert foxes started using their hearing to locate lizards, and foxes with bigger ears found this much easier. The big-eared foxes were the better hunters and the better survivors. Larger ears also helped them regulate their body heat!

The big-eared, short-furred foxes were the best survivors in the desert, so they were the ones who went on to produce offspring. Over multiple generations, those big ear and short fur genes were passed down until we ended up with the small giant-eared foxes we know today as fennec foxes.

The two species are all just foxes at their very core and all came from the same ancestors, but their different environments caused them to change in appearance over time. The individuals with the traits that ensured the best survival in their home were the ones to reproduce and continued passing down those traits to their kits.

Now the two are nearly unrecognizable from each other! Who knows what kind of animals we might see around us in a few hundred years.

ALFRED GOES HOME

Alfred returned from Asia in 1862, he was almost 40 years old. He spent some time visiting Charles Darwin and bonding as friends. He also met a nice wife and had three children, finally settling down and enjoying domestic life with his family.

He shared his love of nature with his children, even letting a lizard run around the study with them while he worked on papers!

PUBLISHING PARTY

Alfred wrote and published many books on a variety of topics. He studied other natural phenomena such as hypnosis and social issues such as feminism. He was also interested in spiritualism (which is the study of ghosts!) and whether life could exist on other planets. He dedicated his life to sharing his ideas and discoveries with the world. In 1908, he was awarded a medal for his life's work, and was very proud of it.

The Darwin-Wallace Medal is still awarded to scientists today for their incredible work on evolutionary discoveries.

Animals, hypnotism, human rights, ghosts, and aliens . . . he was certainly a versatile guy!

THE END FOR ALFRED

Alfred lived a long life, until he was 90 years old! His last books were published in 1913. He died in his sleep, but not before leaving hundreds of studies which helped shape how we see the world of evolution today. Thousands of scientists have built on the ideas he left behind, and there is a statue honoring him in the gardens of London's Natural History Museum—you can still see it there today!

ALFRED'S ANIMALS

Alfred discovered thousands of living things that were previously unknown to science, and he even had some animals named after him, such as Wallace's flying frog, Wallace's jewel beetle, and Wallace's standardwing, a rare bird-of-paradise he found in Indonesia.

That's me!

Obviously all of us animals existed before Alfred documented us, though. In fact, the first time Europe saw a bird like me was in the 16th century when Ferdinand Magellan, the first ever person to sail the circumference of the globe, brought back a few from his journey as gifts for the King of Spain.

CHARLES ROBERT DARWIN

• Born in 1809 to an upper-class family.

• Went on his famous journey from 1831 to 1836.

• His most famous book was called *On the Origin of Species*, which provided evidence and an explanation of evolution.

• Was the first naturalist to visit the Galapagos islands.

• Had the theory of evolution named after him (Darwinism).

• Had over 120 species of animals named after him.

• Convinced the majority of scientists that evolution was real and is known for revolutionizing the way we think about the natural world.

ALFRED RUSSEL WALLACE

• Born in 1823 to a working class family.

• Went on his first journey from 1848 to 1852 to South America, and his second journey from 1854 to 1862 to Indonesia, Malaysia, and Singapore.

• Was involved in a shipwreck and lost years of work.

• Developed the theory of warning colorization.

• Had birds, bugs, frogs, and a faunal boundary line named after him.

• Collected research and made discoveries that made huge contributions to how we understand evolution today, both supporting and building on Darwin's theories.

CRAZY COLLECTORS

When Alfred was 21 years old, he made a new friend at the library named Henry Walter Bates. Henry had an incredible collection of insects, and it inspired Alfred to start his own. The two of them would spend hours hunting the tiny critters together.

Can you find all 14 creepy crawlies hiding on this page?

PUZZLE ANSWERS

WHAT A COLLECTION!

Alfred's journey lasted eight years and he traveled more than 10,000 miles. Over that time, he collected almost 110,000 insects, 7,500 shells, 8,050 bird skins, and 410 mammals. There are nearly 10,000 different species of birds in the world, and Alfred discovered just over 2% of them. That's 246 types of birds that no one had ever documented before!

Some of Alfred's collections have escaped! Can you help by finding them out?

Can you match up which animals on the right you think shared ancestors with the animals on the left?

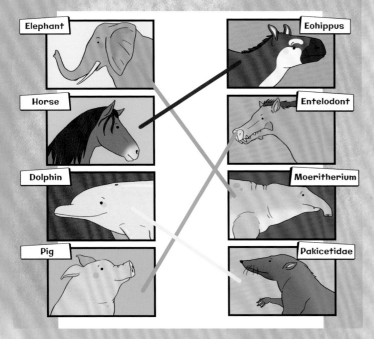

Elephant
Horse
Dolphin
Pig

Eohippus
Entelodont
Moeritherium
Pakicetidae

How many did you find?

The wacky, the funny, and the eccentric, the second ones in the world . . .

The Second in the World
to Sail the Globe: Sir Fransic Drake

Sir Francis Drake, a murderous pirate working for the Queen of England in the 16th century, was the second person ever known to sail around the globe. On a quest to steal treasures, hunt for spices, and annoy the King of Spain as much as possible, Francis and his crew aboard the *Golden Hind* might have not been the first, but they were certainly the wackiest.

The Second in the World
to Discover Evolution: Alfred Russel Wallace

Alfred Russel Wallace, a 19th century naturalist, was the second person in the world known to discover the secrets of evolution. With his epic journey around the world in search of creepy crawlies and flying beasties, fiery ship disasters, and feverish forest findings, Alfred might have not been the first, but he was certainly the most fun.

The Second in the World
to Invent the Telephone: Elisha Gray

Elisha Gray, a dairy farmer turned inventor in the 19th century, came second in the race to invent the telephone—or did he? With his wacky discoveries using bathtub instruments, rich dentists, and electric pianos, Elisha might not been the first, but the story of his discovery was just as eccentric.

YEEHOO PRESS BEST-SELLING AND UPCOMING

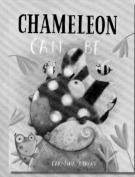

Chameleon Can Be

The Happiest Kid

My Monsterpiece

When I´m Not Looking

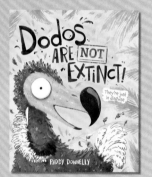

Dodos Are Not Extinct

The Vanishing Lake

The Gentle Bulldozer

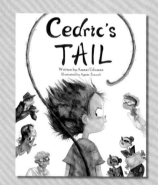

Cedric´s Tall

Piper and Purpa Forever!

The Whole World Inside Nan´s Soup

Milo´s Moonlight Mission

The Perfect Party

Masha Munching

The School of Failure: A Story About Success

Who is it, Whoodini?